Songs of Eela

All rights reserved © Mishka Hajee 2020
No part of the publication may be reproduced, distributed or transmitted in any form or by any means, electronic, mechanical, photocopying, recording, or other, without first obtaining the written permission of the copyright owner, except for the use of brief quotations in reviews.

First published 2020
First edition / 01

Cover illustration copyright © Amy-Jane Jenkins 2020

Author photograph copyright © Misha Lee Tame 2017

ISBN: 978-1-5272-7509-6

www.mishkainthedark.wordpress.com

Songs of Eela

Mishka Hajee

For the one who taught me the meaning of Love
before I took my first breath.
Mom, I love you.

Preface

In twenty-seven years, I have shed more skins than I could have imagined. In some years, I shed several at once and, in others, I lived in old skins for too long.

When Eela was first created, it was not a book of poetry. It was a place of escape, a place to reflect, a place to frolic in the magic of memory. A place to rest my head against a tree and reimagine the world. My world.

Eela has since evolved and is now painted in nostalgia, Love, pain, memory and hope. Eela is the remembrance of stories and lessons, and the realisation that, at times, what may appear to be sentiments caused by external factors, is actually just a projection of sentiment brought about by internal trauma. Maybe the demons aren't outside the house – maybe they live in the skins we keep shelved in the linen closet.

The Songs of Eela contain a recollection of confrontations with the ego, inner dialogue and the past. They push past indulgence towards the middle ground and, finally, awareness.

I'd like to think that I have journeyed through Eela and made my way from self-indulgence to self-awareness. But the truth is, even as I type this in preparation for publication, I am a few skins lighter than I was when I initially decided that the time had come to publish.

The journey through Eela is ongoing. But I hope you enjoy the Songs thus far.

*If creating art is an act of faith,
then let my poetry be a prayer.*

Indulgence & Catharsis

Scars tell stories

My mother's face is young
but her hands, like a leaf, are etched
with cuts and veins and lines
that tell stories –
like the tale of my birth
tattooed behind her left calf
so wherever she goes, she carries me with her.

The tales of Paradise are cracked with grey
I see it in her raised heels after a busy day,
like that of Divine Love and empathy
stories I did not understand
until the day I cut my knees
whilst climbing trees –
when I finally looked down,
I had seen my mother bleed.

I hear her whisper prayers at three A.M.
in the dark, when she thinks we're asleep
but doesn't she know, we see the burns on her hands
from a thava in the kitchen before dawn.
She packs lunches and letters
into Tupperware containers
creating love out of thin air,
band-aids for broken skin.

My mother's eyes hold memory
but she does not count the stories
of battlefields and broken wings.

But I do. I have counted
every scar and feather
every lunchbox letter –
a collection of silent *'I love you'*s
tucked beneath my skin
so that when I cannot run to her
I need simply look in the mirror.

Empty Frame

In a rush to get away and begin a new chapter
I hastily packed my bags,
hid our memories in a box to be left behind
and slid the lessons into my cosmetic case.

But as I packed our picture in a frame
it slipped from my hands.
The thin sheet of ice,
a window of the past,
fragile and light,
shattered
into a hundred shards.

Ice that was meant to numb me
cut my feet until I bled,
and melted away memories I had made –
colours wash away
smiles fade.

Picture perfect
shattered glass
Now all that remains –
an empty frame.

Omission

You lied.

An omission
like a spark
burned through your paper truths,
and your words lie charred
in an ashtray
waiting to be blown away.

Breadcrumbs

I left you breadcrumbs to find
scattered across the mess you left behind.
I blew rose petals in the wind
you set them alight and grinned.

I left footprints in the sand
hoping you'd follow and take my hand.
Instead you wandered down a different path
then came running back in the aftermath.
Your ash-laden hands tried to grab at my dress
a white silken cloak, now a grey mess.

I poured rosewater on your burns
ignored your snide remarks and spurns.
I heard the guilt in your every word, your every line
knowing you should've followed the crumbs I left you to find.

You held onto me until your burns healed
yet there was still pain that could not be concealed;
instead of learning to live with your scars
you sought false freedom behind prison bars.

Away you went and left me alone again
to scatter breadcrumbs like a good friend.

Pretty Lies Rhyme

I liked the way your pretty lies rhyme,
the way your paper words fly.

The way your ashen poems stain my skin,
your verses are deep, but your voice is thin.

The unmeasured notes in the way you sing,
the way your lyrics carry in the winter wind.

Your letters piled on a pyre,
your choices set them on fire.

Black smoke swirls in the air,
choking me and incensing my hair.

You are gone, but the echoes of your pretty lies
are still alive in my eyes.

Ruins

I walk these dusty streets
among deserted castles,
stone walls once built by concrete men
now laid to ruin,
like our paper dreams
lying in shreds and dust
along a long, lonely path.

Chasing the Moon

I spent my nights chasing the moon
whilst you pocketed the stars,
one by one, you plucked them from the sky,
placing them in the inner pocket of your coat.

In an open field
I bathed in the moonlight
baring my skin to the sky
and, all the while,
the stars burned a hole in your pocket
turning to ash in your hands
and your skies darkened.

When I danced in the dark,
glowing with moonbeams,
you mistook me for a star you could pocket.

But the constellations do not trust you
and when you got too close
the moonlight burned your eyes –

that was the day you learned why
it was dangerous to look directly at an eclipse.

Cigarette

The flame licks
the tip of your cigarette,
kissing the paper in its fiery embrace.

The sweet scent of nicotine
as you take her in till your craving is satisfied,
as the red-orange light sears through
leaving nothing
but black
and grey ash
behind.

Carelessly, you throw the stub away.

Friendship's Grave

We disguise our hurt with anger
fickle and frivolous,
its sting is skin deep
its effects, temporary.

Yellow roses dried in self-righteousness,
words turning poems to ashes –
a slow death to this friendship.

Together,
we lowered empty words and broken promises
six feet into the ground
etched the grieving of memories onto a tombstone;
a sore reminder of apathy.

Shadows live in Light

Your shadows lived in my light for too long -
projected self-hate filled the air with smoke
until I choked on the truth.

I took the matchstick you used to set me on fire
and held it to the bridge between us
watching it go up in flames
blinding your gaze
until all that was left was the ocean between us.

Water

And I
I left you
to wonder why
I said goodbye
like a waterfall in a drought -
soft, faint,
a whisper.

Like water you take for granted,
water sliding down your back,
water that cleanses you,
water lets you breathe.

Water
that heals you –
an endless ocean
so submerged within you
it became a part of you.

Water
that you forgot you needed
that you drank every day
without a second thought.

Water
you wasted
while I waited
a patient stream
simmering beneath the surface.

Water
you stirred and sipped
while I bubbled and boiled.

Water
that vaporised
and rose above
and away.

Water
that you now
subconsciously reach for.

You bring the cup to your lips
but it is dry
and you search for moisture
where you left me.

But I have risen –
above
and away.

Qismat

Every book has a final chapter
Every fable, an ending –
you and I threaded together across oceans
held only by sentiments and memories.

When we held on for too long
the thread between us cut through our fingers,
leaving blood on our hands.
Qismat is swift and sudden,
more powerful than you and I,
and when we tried to fight her
we set ourselves on fire.

Spitting fire through my teeth

There is a flame in the pit of my stomach
and my soul is a candle Wick
within a Lantern.

Yet the words I want to say
push past the charcoal in my chest,
get caught in my throat
and I choke on the Truth.

So, instead of glowing in darkness,
I spit fire through my teeth
burning everything around me.

Mirror Mermaid

I once saw a mermaid trapped beneath the surface of a lake

She stared back at me through mermaid tears,
her outstretched hands tried to push past the water's surface
her tail thrashing violently.

But she was imprisoned by the same water which gave her life.
She began to sing, and though she was trapped,
her sweet melancholy echoed in ripples across the surface.

I turned away and left my reflection behind
trapped beneath the surface of the water.

Corazón

Heartbeat against the palm of my hand
caught between a wall and a hard place
each pulse the sound of a liar,
the drumbeat of deceitful desire.

Corazón

Sweet, sweet melancholy swim in your eyes
Water turns black to grey
and I cannot see past the lies –
so I let you have your way.

Corazón

Water turns to paraffin and I ignite
I set myself on fire to bring you light
Clicking fingers to a steady heartbeat
a flint sparks the fire, and all I feel is heat.

Corazón

You took my serotonin and dopamine
and made music with a tambourine
water beating on a drum, blood on my hands –
you left me in darkness, with no one who understands.

Blood

I tried to grow flowers
in the space where my heart
had been uprooted.

But where blood forsakes blood,
there is no water to breathe life.

Ghosts

Ghosts of the past are just lucid air,
yet they cut you like glass
from the mirror into which you look.

Ghosts of the past should remain in closed chapters
yet they haunt you
as inconvenient plot twists.

Ghosts of the past are intangible
yet their fingers claw around your throat,
choking you.

Ghosts of the past are impalpable
yet they leave the bitter aftertaste
of blood in your mouth.

Ghosts of the past swim in the dark depths of your eyes
yet they stare back at you
as truth
from the shattered mirror.

Ego

Trying to unroot my ego
feels like trying to pull hot coals out my throat —

do I give up and give in,
or do I fight back?

Regardless,
I burn.

You buried it

Life handed you a bleeding seed,
and deep down,
in the depths of your chest,
you sowed it.

There it remained,
unnoticed for so long.
Quietly,
deep beneath the soil
it sprouted roots,
growing.

It murmured now and then,
but you were deafened by the chirps
of birds flying overhead
and you didn't hear the lies.
You cast your eyes to the skies
and did not see the vines –

until one day the earth shook
and it burst forth,
like a hot spring –
searing everything in its path.

Cracked Jug

Last night I was a cracked jug,
water trickling out
the fractures of my body,
my elbows hugging my ribs.

Last night
I was broken, but full.

                                  Last night I was tipped over,
                                  violently turned onto my side
                                  water pouring onto the tablecloth
                                  drenching it.

                                  Last night
                                  I was unbroken,
                                  but finally
                                  empty.

I wish the darkness in me would stop screaming your name.

"Sin with me"

Sin is sweet and unsatisfying.
Sin is temporary
a spark slowly dying.

Sin is the flame
kissing the cigarette.
Sin is a game
ensnaring one in its net.

Sin might be raw
Sin might be pure –
but sin is fire
burning
destructive
leaving grey ash
to blow carelessly to the floor.

Steel scarves

Steel scarves,
cold, calculated, confining,
spring from the ground like vines
and snake around my ankles
rooting me in place,

snake around my arms
shackling my wrists,

snake around my throat
choking me.

I cannot breathe in this steel cage
that I so willingly stepped into.

Mud

We cleanse ourselves in the ash of our actions
under the delusion that mud erases mud,
leaving ourselves covered in dirt and water
the caking of ash and tears,
allowing for moss to grow over
and forgetting that the mud was there.

We sink deeper into the ground
quicksand around our ankles
seductively tugging us in
before we cleanse ourselves with holy fire.

Middle Ground

Barrier

Sometimes
the heart is the barrier
between you and the Truth
that has to be broken
for you to remember
the song of your soul.

Pool of Blood

That fateful autumn, the dried band aids were finally ripped off my wounds, revealing sores that did not heal when I tried to run. As I bled, the darkness within me was being stripped away. It was only when I lay in a pool of my own blood, when my hair, bloodied black, stuck to my head and shoulders, that I was forced to sit still.

A love letter to my insecurities

The night before your flight out of town,
in the witness of the rain and thunder,
you tried to kiss me one last time to remind me
of the taste of ash on my tongue
but my lips remained sealed.

I forced you into silence
by confronting you with the truth,
brought you back to the path
when you tried to misguide my thoughts.
I took the power out of your hands
and that was when you realised you no longer
have a home here.

I did not message to check if you got home safe that night.

Girl of the Earth

Dear Girl of the Earth
Hair as brown as tree roots
Eyes set ablaze by sunlight
the smile of sunflowers
the innocence of a rosebud.

When they put up a barbed-wire fence around you,
you mistook protection for imprisonment
love for cruelty –
fresh soil is naïve
the old willow would know.

It is easy to mistake a balloon vine,
an alien invader,
for a friendly fern.
You took no notice when the balloon vine
twisted its way around the barbed-wire,
into your soil
and began to grow a home.

Girl of Dust,
there is smoke in your eyes
you have forgotten the colours of the skies.
Why are you pouring ocean water into cigarette ash
hoping to grow tulips?

I watch the forest pass through Autumn
it has grown quiet here,
save for the yellow-orange leaves that fall –
the balloon vine set itself alight, crumpled up
and blew away with the winter winds.

Girl of the Forest,
I see ivy leaves climbing up the bark of trees
a rooted spine holding your history
on each leaf, a memory.

Don't hide behind leaved curtains in regret
and forget
that there is nothing wrong with a good intention
should I mention
the lessons
you unearthed the day you ripped out your rooted ego
and began to plant daisies.

You finally learnt, nymph of the forest,
guarding your heart is not self-interest.

Look up, Girl of the Earth.
The sunlight pushes past the trees
and sets your forest aglow.

Go now,
and bathe in the warm sunlight.

She wronged

She wronged
He wronged
You wronged
I wronged
and you wronged again.

She wronged
He wronged
They wronged
You wronged
I wronged
You wronged again.

She keeps wronging
He's always wrong
Their wrongs are written
too deep.
So you wrong and I wrong
and you wrong me again
in water and red.

There are no rights in these wrongs
It's only wrong, wrong, wrong.

Yet, in your wrongs there was a right
There were still wrongs, but the right was light
And the Wick lit up
in the darkness of wrongs.

I forgive you.

Red-Orange and Crystal-Blue

You look at me
and all I see
is light trapped behind your eyes
trying to fight its way past the lies.
Yet you choose to be fire
you place fragments of yourself on a pyre.
Instead of letting light weld your soul
you set alight the remnants – leaving behind a hole.

I am ocean, I am sea, I am water
I am waves in the wind, I am Poseidon's daughter.

I would not douse your fire
lest you multiply your desire,
I choose only to reflect your light
that which you keep hidden out of sight.
You are much more than red-orange flame
you are light refracted, a rainbow untamed.
If released, your light would be blinding
Sunlight through the trees, energy unwinding.

I look into you and you look into me
fire and light meet the crystal-blue sea,
no matter which wins out, the old mermaid knows
despite the raging fire, there is still a light that glows.

Black Ink

Setting old diaries and letters alight
does not erase the mistakes, the memories,
the imprinted histories.

So why am I standing here with a blowtorch
ready to burn down a forest?

Perhaps if I mix the ashes
together with my tears
I will be left with black ink
to write a new tale.

Vulnerability

Like a tree in the dead of winter,
you are just as beautiful
when you are bare.

Something Stirred

Something stirred
in the depths of the forest
buried deep
beneath cracks of hardened soil.

Something stirred
behind thorny vines
and prickly pines,
and a barbed wire fence.

Under dried purple orchard petals
among fields of
deeply rooted red tulips,
where sunlight is guarded by sheets of grey.

Something stirred.

She climbed carefully over
the barbed wire,
her footprints feint in the dry earth
past thorny vines
and prickly pines;
orchard petals crush
and become dust
under her weight
as she lay amongst the soft red tulips.

Eyes scan the skies,
she waits for a downpour of sunlight;
though she is surrounded by red
her focus is on the feint purple instead.

And she too felt it.

Beneath the cracked earth
under dried crushed orchard petals,

Something stirred.

Nostalgia

I opened a page from a storybook of the past
and began to miss our adventures,
and, in a swirl of nostalgia, I almost reached out to you.

But the burns you left on the back of my right hand
reminded me to close the book.

Grey

In challenging ourselves we understand
that we are simply human beings,
a mixture of light and darkness,
attempting to navigate life
along a tightrope of grey.

Sing

While the world screams in bright colours,
I sing Your Name in darkness.

And that is how I remember
to breathe again.

Watercolours

If you and I are no longer meant to be
why do I meet you in watercolour dreams
behind my eyelids
dissolving when I awake?

Our last conversation in the car
the day I knew you'd gone too far
driving along the shoreline
pretending everything was fine.

My love – don't you see the mess you've left behind?

Polaroids of birthday cake and fading candles
you promised you always had my back
held my hand, pulling me down the promised path –
I was blinded by your red-orange hue
but you bled me out till I was blue.

Time runs like water across these painted scenes
and they begin the fade, over time and space
to days
when I don't remember your face.

So why do I wake up at night to echoes of your name?

Roots

We wear our roots on our sleeves
veins on our forearms filled with the blood of our ancestors
orphans hidden on boats across the Indian Ocean
married into foreign lands
culling sugarcane in fields
building empires from dust
learning new cultures and tongues
trying to plant old roots in foreign soil.

We are the descendants of diaspora,
the progeny of indentured labourers and merchants
taught to survive when, what we want, is to live.

We carry their legacy
whilst laying down our own.

Birdhouse

At the centre of farmlands of old
there is a fragile little birdhouse
that blows & twists in the wind.

Every day the winds try to break the nest
fate threatens to unravel meshed leaves in a mess
but Faith Holds it together.

Flock migration moved south for the winter
but a little family of birds stayed,
beating broken wings against the sky
knowing Spring would bear her flowers.

In a simple little birdhouse
whenever the wind blows
Faith keeps these birds fighting
in their one-and-a-half-bedroom home.

*I forgot You
and in doing so,
I forgot myself.*

Long Distance

I awoke last night
city lights and pretty nights
behind my eyes,
and I yearned for those stone-structured memories
you had built three years ago.

London

London was diverse enough to make me feel at home
and I grew comfortable in her many skins.

London had hooks in every corner to hang up my cloaks –
skins of my own that needed to be discarded.

I left my cloak of naïveté in a hidden corner in Canary Wharf
between the DLR and the Thames
where yellow-orange sunrises sparkle through glass buildings
if you're early enough to catch the morning train.

Every year I revisit this corner
but never again try on the cloak –
nostalgia is exquisite
but sentiment can be cruel.

The parakeets in Kensington Gardens carried away judgement
a cloak I thought I had once shed,
but London's colours, that scream within Banksy Tunnel,
glimmering in the nightlife,
taught me otherwise.

In a city where midnight strolls
with mates on London Bridge
turned into early mornings in Shoreditch,
I left my cloak of banality on a red bus
whilst trying to make my way back home.

After I broke my fast
with strangers in Malet Street Gardens,
I got on the tube at Goodge Street
and followed the Northern Line to Golders Green.

I got lost in the crowd
between bookworms and businessmen,
artists and tourists -
I made no eye contact,
but I knew I belonged.

In her many skins,
London made shedding my own seem more acceptable
and shed I did, until I remembered
who I was
and who I was not.

Each time I return, I am a different person –
but London remembers me anyway.

Kite

I was a kite
free and light
letting life's winds
push
and pull
and tug
and carry me
up and away
until my legs no longer touched the earth.

I flew too high
and got lost amongst the clouds.
I took no notice of the thorns beneath me
and when I least expected it
a tree branch grabbed my leg
and reeled me back to the ground –
an obstacle
a lesson
a Blessing.

A tale of fire and earth

The bond between fire and earth
runs deeper than campfires and forests –
elements connected in nature and spirit
yet fire chose percussion and destruction
while earth grew silent and heard
the echoes of Truth
like waterfalls
pouring down the edges of cliffs.

Earth provided trees for the fire to stretch and grow
and fire left earth with stumps and dead tree bark –
that was when earth learned
not to expect fire to love earth more
than earth loves herself.

Earth buried fire deep beneath the sand now
the crackles and whizzes don't sound out anymore
because even veld fires,
once they've raged their loudest,
fall silent when they return to the earth.

Seagulls on rooftops

When the sky burns red
and I long for the Fajr and Maghrib song
of the birds of Westville,
God sends me seagulls atop Dublin City rooftops
echoes of Love sound across the city skyline
and,
in that moment,
I know I am home.

Actualisation

&

Awareness

Storm

I know right now you are weathering a storm –
but darling,
have you ever noticed when the rain stops
how the streets glisten in the sunlight?

Unopened box

Passing by a park in our childhood town
where you once said you would meet me,
I sit on a bench
beneath the wild fig tree
and wonder what would have happened
if you and I opened our shared toy box.

Would it have burst open with starlight,
the two of us spinning in the sky –
would the constellations have sounded approving sighs.
Would it have played out like the songs and tales –
the birth of young love under front yard hedges.
Would my voice have grown so intertwined with yours
that I would never know the sound of my own melody;
how powerfully it sounds over the din of expectations.

Or,

Would it have unleashed a tempest of violent love,
the soundtrack of percussion and ash.
Would the pixies have turned to púca
as I unearthed insecurities I had yet to uncover.
Would I have been heartbroken by the discovery
of the idea of love, an escapism for clinical reality.

I was alone that day, beneath the wild fig tree
with a sealed toy box to bury in the sand.

Knowing that we both bathe in light, I know it turned out okay,
I understand it was Fate that you did not show up that day.

Petrified

The knot tightens
The ache spreads, then stops,
spreads, then stops.
These thoughts, these words
these actions.

Surrounded by colour
yet all I see is black and white.
Grey dust clouds my path
but the end is in sight.

Blood, sweat, tears
Blood, sweat, fears.
My cries, my pleas; You Hear.
In the midst of uncertainty, You're Near.

The knot loosens
These thoughts know
These words flow
These actions grow.

Fearless

High school science class cupboard

You cannot force a plant to grow in the sunlight
when he chooses to keep himself
in a high school science class cupboard.

You cannot force feed him chlorophyll
and expect him to grow like front yard ferns.

Do not be angry when he rejects the light
and twists into colourless stems,
then hold yourself accountable
when he gets tangled within himself.

His pre-conditioning is not your responsibility to fix
his actions are not yours to rectify –

you cannot change the nature of a man
who does not want to change.

Stop sticking your hand
into that high school science class cupboard
trying to uproot a seed already deep-rooted in darkness.

And,
instead,
begin to revel in your own Light.

Archway

I am ready to write a new chapter
but blood stains and spring rains
keep seeping through the pages.

Gluing the pages together don't keep out old resentments
so I tried to send you an olive branch on the back of a lapwing.

The walls I put up to protect myself have not crumbled,
but I have decided to leave the door open now
– not for you to walk in,
but rather for me to stand in the archway
and wave
as you pass by.

The Woman

You are a tree standing tall
feet rooted into the ground
hands outstretched towards the sky,
carrying yourself
and others
with quiet strength and wisdom.

Who convinced you
that a man was physically stronger than you
when it is your hips that crack when bearing life.

Show me a heart that is stronger
than that of the ones who are torn in two
whilst bringing new life into this world
and giving off nothing but love.

Why did you let men convince you
that your inclination
towards emotion
makes you weak –
when did the definition
of feeling encompass
faults and flaws,
the very essence of what makes us
human
held against you –
like a thorn intended to cut you.

Their loose lips lash out at you
but you sharpen your tongue on the rocks they threw –
they forgot the rose has thorns too.

You are greenery
growing through the cracks in the sidewalk
tearing through the darkness
stretching towards the sun.

Physics of light

An open heart is a window with the curtains drawn
receiving Love,

refracting every spectrum
of Light.

Dhikr

is the silencing of the mind,
to listen to the heart,
to bring peace to the soul.

Adelaide Road

I turn right on Adelaide Road
coming up on Harcourt Street
towards St. Stephen's Green –
and wonder if you see me
as clearly as I see you.

When we first met, I painted you
in pre-conceived colours,
I mistook you for a former lover
and as the leaves on the trees
in St. Stephen's Green
turned to red and yellow
we fought.

When the leaves finally fell
and winter breathed her cold morning air
I wanted to leave.

But winter soon turned to spring,
your eyes softened and,
finally
I began to see your spectrum of colours
and recognised them as my own.

Your gentle rains
                      My growing pains
Our narratives began to intertwine.

Your green embrace
                      ignored my past mistakes
and I began to wonder if you were mine.

Do you recognise me
through your grey-green eyes?
Can you spot me in the crowds
around the buskers on Grafton Street?

Or am I just another face passing by
on Adelaide Road
late night on the Airlink bus
trying to make my way back home.

Daisies

You Plant daises for me to find
along the path You Want me to take.
But for the longest time I was blinded by smoke
and could not see the clearing in front of me.

Now I string the daisies along a chain and wear them in my hair.

The dance

Perhaps life is a dance
between the realms of Knowing
and Unknowing
ourselves.

Salaah –

a celebration of Unity
between the Divine
and His Beloved.

Whenever life cracks open your heart, I pray that you bleed love.

Cape Town – a city made for love

We sat on bronze and granite that September
ice cream dripping down our hands –
do you remember
secret meetings and stolen glances
on Devil's Peak, when morning hikes
turned to late night drives.

We saw the lights stretched out across Cape Town city
You held my hand and said the lights weren't as pretty
as my eyes in the low light
blinking back at you that September night.

Back when we were young
and thought we had it figured out,
trying to catch the future in our hands
because we watched our pasts slip through our fingers;

But I like the way yours fit between mine
when we walked along the shoreline.

Desert girl

She wanders through the desert
parched
her knees drag through the sand
pouring down the hourglass.

You Pour a full jug
into her glass
every drop
a Mercy.

The glass overflows.

Cold Winds

When turbulence rocked the plane
when St. Stephen's Green was drenched in rain
when winter's winds howled against my windowpane,
back when I thought there was nothing left to gain –

when the cold wind stung me, like bees in a hive,
that was when I felt most alive.

Veil on the shoreline

I trudged along the coast
in a wedding dress
looking for the boat
that was to bring me home.

In my mind, the waves churned
and I cried out loud;
My love,
do the world's winds and whirlwinds carry my voice
to you
or do they drown it out?

I raised my head up to the sky
desperately looking for a sign
pacing back and forth along the shoreline
trying to surrender to Divine Time.

I kicked the sand in despair
and watched the waves retreat
hoping that, one day soon,
I'll return home to you.

My wet veil stuck to the sand,
holding me in place;
my world between the waves
as I waited for a boat that never came
and I wondered how long until I see you again.

Glossary

Thava	A flat pan used in Indian households, often to make roti.
Qismat	Fate, destiny.
Fajr	Early morning prayer.
Maghrib	Prayer after sunset.
Dhikr	Remembrance of God.
Salaah	Prayer.
Veld	Open grassland in Southern Africa.
Corazón	A Spanish word, referring to the heart or spirit, often used as a term of endearment.
Púca	A creature of Celtic folklore.

Acknowledgements

A special thank you to Misha Lee Tame and Amy Jane Jenkins who turned my daydreams into a visual reality with photography and watercolours.

Thank you to my teachers Mev. C. Herselman and Mrs. M. Reddy of Westville Girls' High School for sparking my interest in writing and poetry during my high school years.

A special thank you to the following people who have provided valuable insight and encouragement over the years:

Shabbir Banoobhai, Nafisa Hansa, Farzanah Mall, Priyanka Naidoo, Aneesa Mahomed, Aisha Hamdulay and Ejaz Khan.

Thank you to Ebrahim Shaikh for making the things that terrify me seemingly less terrifying, and for always reminding me of my dreams when I have forgotten them – I hope, one day soon, I'll be coming home to you.

Thank you to my father, Cassim Hajee, whose love for qawalli and dhikr I have grown to appreciate as I've gotten older. I miss our car rides on the way to school.

Thank you to my sister, Ridwa Hajee, who would always read my unfinished short stories and daydreams when we were kids, without my permission, and then promptly demand to read the rest – you have always been the first member of my audience.

Thank you to my mother, Razia Norath, for always feeding my creativity, encouraging me to take Dramatic Arts instead of Biology in high school and for your continued patience. I can't imagine that it has been easy bringing up two strong-headed young women in a society where our roles come with its own preconceived terms and conditions – thank you for not allowing outside voices to dictate our stories and for being the strength of our little birdhouse. I love you.

Mishka Hajee is a chartered accountant and creative writer who has taken inspiration from other like-minded professionals in her home country, South Africa.

After undertaking the seven-year journey of qualifying as a chartered accountant in South Africa, Mishka decided to spend some time abroad while she figures out how to marry her professional qualification with her creativity. She currently resides in the Republic of Ireland. *Songs of Eela* is her first published collection of poetry.

Printed by Amazon Italia Logistica S.r.l.
Torrazza Piemonte (TO), Italy